Gratitude
A to Z
Journal

by Tracy Fagan

Copyright © 2016 by Tracy Fagan

Interior and Exterior Design: Tracy Fagan
Illustrations: nightwolfdezines

All rights reserved. This book or any portion thereof may not be reproduced or used in any manner, digital or physical, whatsoever without the express written permission of the publisher except for the use of brief quotations in a book review.

Scripture quotations are from the ESV® Bible (The Holy Bible, English Standard Version®), copyright © 2001 by Crossway, a publishing ministry of Good News Publishers. Used by permission. All rights reserved.

Printed in the United States of America

ISBN-13: 978-0692610503

Fireball Creative
PO Box 653
Parker, CO 80134

www.FireballCreative.net

This book is dedicated to
my Lord and Savior, Jesus Christ.
Without such an amazing God, we would have
nothing to be thankful for.

Table of Contents

How to Use this Book........9
A.............................10
B.............................12
C.............................14
D.............................16
E.............................18
F.............................20
G.............................22
H.............................24
I.............................26
J.............................28
K.............................30
L.............................32
M.............................34
N.............................36
O.............................38
P.............................40
Q.............................42
R.............................44
S.............................46
T.............................48
U.............................50
V.............................52
W.............................54
X.............................56
Y.............................58
Z.............................60
Observations.................62
Alphabet Strips..............65

colors ~ people ~ places ~ things ~ food   ~ books ~ smells ~ movies ~ activities

This journal belongs to:

Date(s) of journaling:

How to use this Book

Have you ever played "The Alphabet Game" while driving in the car? You know, where you go through the alphabet looking for a specific letter on signs or license plates. It is a great way to pass the time, but it also requires you to actively look with anticipation for a certain letter. This books encourages you to increase your gratitude by using the challenge of seeking people, places and things starting with a specific letter in which you are grateful. This is a unique way to help you think about what you are thinking about – and help you focus on gratitude.

So think of this book like the alphabet game, but "driving" through your life, seeking things you are grateful for.

There is no right or wrong way to use this book. If you are looking for a twist, here are some creative suggestions -

- » Take a letter a day and move through the book A to Z
- » Take a letter a day and move through the book Z to A
- » Add items to the appropriate letter when they come to mind
- » Pull a random letter out of a jar and focus on that letter for the day (see pg. 65 for creating letter strips. You supply the jar.)
- » Make it a family affair - pick one letter per night and have everyone take turns contributing items that begin with that letter
- » For holidays or family dinners, have each person pick their own letter and share his/her gratitude with the group
- » Apply alliteration to all letters of the alphabet. Be amazed at your awesomness!

Remember, the goal is to increase your gratitude.
Have fun. Be grateful! Enjoy!

A

colors ~ people ~ places ~ things ~ food ~ { 10 } ~ books ~ smells ~ movies ~ activities

Give thanks in **A**ll circumstances;
for this is the will of God in Christ Jesus for you.
1 Thessalonians 5:18 ESV

colors ~ people ~ places ~ things ~ food ~   ~ books ~ smells ~ movies ~ activities

colors ~ people ~ places ~ things ~ food ~   { 12 }   ~ books ~ smells ~ movies ~ activities

colors ~ people ~ places ~ things ~ food ~   { 13 }   ~ books ~ smells ~ movies ~ activities

colors ~ people ~ places ~ things ~ food   { 14 }   ~ books ~ smells ~ movies ~ activities

On the recollection of so many and great favours and Blessings, I now, with a high sense of gratitude, presume to offer up my sincere thanks to the Almighty, the Creator and Preserver.
~ *William Bartram*

colors ~ people ~ places ~ things ~ food ~   { 15 }   ~ books ~ smells ~ movies ~ activities

colors ~ people ~ places ~ things ~ food ~ { 16 } ~ books ~ smells ~ movies ~ activities

colors ~ people ~ places ~ things ~ food ~   [**17**]   ~ books ~ smells ~ movies ~ activities

colors ~ people ~ places ~ things ~ food ~ { 18 } ~ books ~ smells ~ movies ~ activities

Counting your blessings is the ultimate attitude adjuster.
If you find yourself in a bad mood or being critical of things in your life, begin to *C*ount your blessings.
Continue until you notice the shift in the atmosphere.

colors ~ people ~ places ~ things ~ food ~   ~ books ~ smells ~ movies ~ activities

colors ~ people ~ places ~ things ~ food ~ { 20 } ~ books ~ smells ~ movies ~ activities

colors ~ people ~ places ~ things ~ food ~   { 21 }   ~ books ~ smells ~ movies ~ activities

colors ~ people ~ places ~ things ~ food ~ { 22 } ~ books ~ smells ~ movies ~ activities

This is the **D**ay that the Lord has made;
let us rejoice and be glad in it.
Psalm 118:24 ESV

colors ~ people ~ places ~ things ~ food ~   { 23 }   ~ books ~ smells ~ movies ~ activities

colors ~ people ~ places ~ things ~ food ~   { 24 }   ~ books ~ smells ~ movies ~ activities

colors ~ people ~ places ~ things ~ food ~   { 25 }   ~ books ~ smells ~ movies ~ activities

colors ~ people ~ places ~ things ~ food ~   { 26 }   ~ books ~ smells ~ movies ~ activities

One of my favorite feelings are spring and summer Evenings, when the chill in the air is just enough to require a sweatshirt... while still wearing shorts.

colors ~ people ~ places ~ things ~ food ~   ~ books ~ smells ~ movies ~ activities

colors ~ people ~ places ~ things ~ food ~   { 28 }   ~ books ~ smells ~ movies ~ activities

colors ~ people ~ places ~ things ~ food ~   ~ books ~ smells ~ movies ~ activities

colors ~ people ~ places ~ things ~ food ~ { 30 } ~ books ~ smells ~ movies ~ activities

Failure is only failure if you refuse to learn from it.
Be thankful for the opportunity to grow.

colors ~ people ~ places ~ things ~ food ~   { 31 }   ~ books ~ smells ~ movies ~ activities

colors ~ people ~ places ~ things ~ food ~ { 32 } ~ books ~ smells ~ movies ~ activities

colors ~ people ~ places ~ things ~ food ~   { 33 }   ~ books ~ smells ~ movies ~ activities

colors ~ people ~ places ~ things ~ food ~   { 34 }   ~ books ~ smells ~ movies ~ activities

Every good Gift and every perfect Gift is from above, coming down from the Father of lights with whom there is no variation or shadow due to change.
James 1:17 ESV

colors ~ people ~ places ~ things ~ food ~   ~ books ~ smells ~ movies ~ activities

colors ~ people ~ places ~ things ~ food ~ { 36 } ~ books ~ smells ~ movies ~ activities

H

colors ~ people ~ places ~ things ~ food ~   ~ books ~ smells ~ movies ~ activities

What does **H**eaven on earth look like to you?

colors ~ people ~ places ~ things ~ food ~   ~ books ~ smells ~ movies ~ activities

colors ~ people ~ places ~ things ~ food ~   { 41 }   ~ books ~ smells ~ movies ~ activities

I

colors ~ people ~ places ~ things ~ food ~ { 42 } ~ books ~ smells ~ movies ~ activities

Even though sometimes God's Instructions don't seem to be the most logical or fun; they are a blessing from the creator to keep us and bring us much joy!

colors ~ people ~ places ~ things ~ food ~   ~ books ~ smells ~ movies ~ activities

colors ~ people ~ places ~ things ~ food ~   { 44 }   ~ books ~ smells ~ movies ~ activities

colors ~ people ~ places ~ things ~ food ~   { 45 }   ~ books ~ smells ~ movies ~ activities

colors ~ people ~ places ~ things ~ food ~   { 46 }   ~ books ~ smells ~ movies ~ activities

Joy: the expression or display of glad feeling; festive gaiety; a state of happiness or felicity.

colors ~ people ~ places ~ things ~ food ~   { 47 }   ~ books ~ smells ~ movies ~ activities

colors ~ people ~ places ~ things ~ food ~   { 48 }   ~ books ~ smells ~ movies ~ activities

colors ~ people ~ places ~ things ~ food ~ { 49 } ~ books ~ smells ~ movies ~ activities

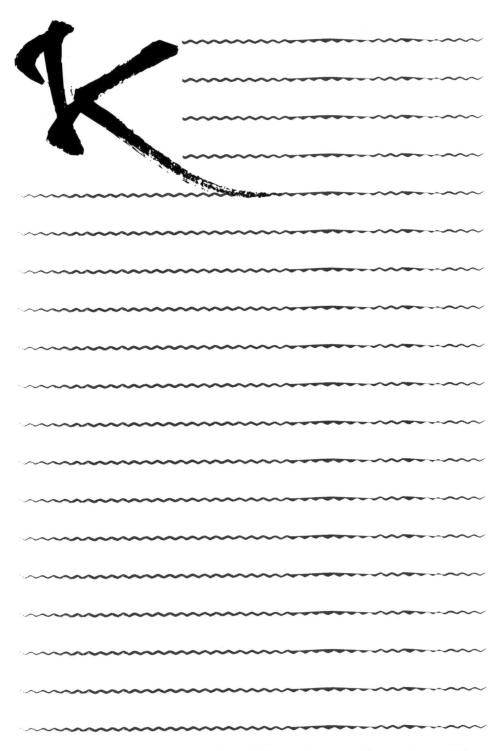

colors ~ people ~ places ~ things ~ food ~   { 50 }   ~ books ~ smells ~ movies ~ activities

Have you ever noticed how a purposeful act of **K**indness can positively impact your life just as much, if not more than the recipient? Try it!

colors ~ people ~ places ~ things ~ food ~   ~ books ~ smells ~ movies ~ activities

colors ~ people ~ places ~ things ~ food ~   { 52 }   ~ books ~ smells ~ movies ~ activities

colors ~ people ~ places ~ things ~ food ~   { 53 }   ~ books ~ smells ~ movies ~ activities

colors ~ people ~ places ~ things ~ food ~ { 54 } ~ books ~ smells ~ movies ~ activities

Oh give thanks to the Lord, for He is good;
for His steadfast love endures forever!
Psalm 107:1 ESV

colors ~ people ~ places ~ things ~ food ~   ~ books ~ smells ~ movies ~ activities

colors ~ people ~ places ~ things ~ food ~   ~ books ~ smells ~ movies ~ activities

colors ~ people ~ places ~ things ~ food ~   { 57 }   ~ books ~ smells ~ movies ~ activities

m

colors ~ people ~ places ~ things ~ food ~ { 58 } ~ books ~ smells ~ movies ~ activities

Prepare your mind and open your eyes to see the *M*iracles
that are happening all around you!

colors ~ people ~ places ~ things ~ food ~   { 59 }   ~ books ~ smells ~ movies ~ activities

colors ~ people ~ places ~ things ~ food ~   { 60 }   ~ books ~ smells ~ movies ~ activities

colors ~ people ~ places ~ things ~ food ~   { 61 }   ~ books ~ smells ~ movies ~ activities

colors ~ people ~ places ~ things ~ food ~ { 62 } ~ books ~ smells ~ movies ~ activities

Have you ever stopped to watch the beauty of Nature?
Take a moment to ponder the delicate intricacies of a flower,
the transformation of a butterfly, or the strength of an ant.

colors ~ people ~ places ~ things ~ food ~   ~ books ~ smells ~ movies ~ activities

colors ~ people ~ places ~ things ~ food ~   { 64 }   ~ books ~ smells ~ movies ~ activities

colors ~ people ~ places ~ things ~ food ~   { 65 }   ~ books ~ smells ~ movies ~ activities

colors ~ people ~ places ~ things ~ food ~   { 66 }   ~ books ~ smells ~ movies ~ activities

Give thanks for your Obstacles. They are not there to end your journey, but make your story more interesting.

colors ~ people ~ places ~ things ~ food ~   { 67 }   ~ books ~ smells ~ movies ~ activities

colors ~ people ~ places ~ things ~ food ~   { 68 }   ~ books ~ smells ~ movies ~ activities

colors ~ people ~ places ~ things ~ food ~   ~ books ~ smells ~ movies ~ activities

P

colors ~ people ~ places ~ things ~ food ~ { 70 } ~ books ~ smells ~ movies ~ activities

And let the Peace of Christ rule in your hearts, to which indeed you were called in one body. And be thankful.
Colossians 3:15 ESV

colors ~ people ~ places ~ things ~ food ~ ~ books ~ smells ~ movies ~ activities

colors ~ people ~ places ~ things ~ food ~   { 72 }   ~ books ~ smells ~ movies ~ activities

colors ~ people ~ places ~ things ~ food ~   { 73 }   ~ books ~ smells ~ movies ~ activities

colors ~ people ~ places ~ things ~ food ~   { 74 }   ~ books ~ smells ~ movies ~ activities

Get out of your funk Quick!
Begin to give thanks for all that you have!

colors ~ people ~ places ~ things ~ food ~   { 75 }   ~ books ~ smells ~ movies ~ activities

colors ~ people ~ places ~ things ~ food ~   { 76 }   ~ books ~ smells ~ movies ~ activities

colors ~ people ~ places ~ things ~ food ~   { 77 }   ~ books ~ smells ~ movies ~ activities

R

colors ~ people ~ places ~ things ~ food ~   { 78 }   ~ books ~ smells ~ movies ~ activities

Remember with fondness those who have Rekindled the
flame of hope in your life.
Step out and have that same impact on someone else.

colors ~ people ~ places ~ things ~ food ~   ~ books ~ smells ~ movies ~ activities

colors ~ people ~ places ~ things ~ food ~   ~ books ~ smells ~ movies ~ activities

colors ~ people ~ places ~ things ~ food ~   { 81 }   ~ books ~ smells ~ movies ~ activities

So

colors ~ people ~ places ~ things ~ food ~ ~ books ~ smells ~ movies ~ activities

It never ceases to amaze me how quickly a Smile can change the atmosphere. It is a free gift that is easy to give and makes a world of difference.

colors ~ people ~ places ~ things ~ food ~   ~ books ~ smells ~ movies ~ activities

colors ~ people ~ places ~ things ~ food ~   { 84 }   ~ books ~ smells ~ movies ~ activities

colors ~ people ~ places ~ things ~ food ~   { 85 }   ~ books ~ smells ~ movies ~ activities

colors ~ people ~ places ~ things ~ food ~ books ~ smells ~ movies ~ activities

Have you ever stopped and thought about the impact
Teachers have on your life?
Which one has had the biggest impact?
Think of one you disliked; what lesson did you learn from them?

colors ~ people ~ places ~ things ~ food ~   { 88 }   ~ books ~ smells ~ movies ~ activities

colors ~ people ~ places ~ things ~ food ~   { 90 }   ~ books ~ smells ~ movies ~ activities

Celebrate the **U**niqueness of every person you experience.
We are all fearfully and wonderfully made by God.

colors ~ people ~ places ~ things ~ food ~ ~ books ~ smells ~ movies ~ activities

colors ~ people ~ places ~ things ~ food ~   { 92 }   ~ books ~ smells ~ movies ~ activities

colors ~ people ~ places ~ things ~ food ~   { 93 }   ~ books ~ smells ~ movies ~ activities

V

colors ~ people ~ places ~ things ~ food ~   { 94 }   ~ books ~ smells ~ movies ~ activities

Thank you to our **V**eterans.
Here is to the men and women — and their families —
who have chosen to serve and protect this great country.

colors ~ people ~ places ~ things ~ food ~   ~ books ~ smells ~ movies ~ activities

colors ~ people ~ places ~ things ~ food ~   ~ books ~ smells ~ movies ~ activities

colors ~ people ~ places ~ things ~ food ~ { 97 } ~ books ~ smells ~ movies ~ activities

W

colors ~ people ~ places ~ things ~ food   { 98 }   ~ books ~ smells ~ movies ~ activities

When the sun rises every morning and the seasons come and go on schedule, I stand in Wonderment of the faithfulness of God.

colors ~ people ~ places ~ things ~ food ~ ~ books ~ smells ~ movies ~ activities

colors ~ people ~ places ~ things ~ food ~ { 100 } ~ books ~ smells ~ movies ~ activities

colors ~ people ~ places ~ things ~ food ~   { **101** }   ~ books ~ smells ~ movies ~ activities

colors ~ people ~ places ~ things ~ food   { 102 }   ~ books ~ smells ~ movies ~ activities

Everyday Life ✘ Gratitude = **Extraordinary Experience**

colors ~ people ~ places ~ things ~ food ~ { 103 } ~ books ~ smells ~ movies ~ activities

colors ~ people ~ places ~ things ~ food ~   { 104 }   ~ books ~ smells ~ movies ~ activities

colors ~ people ~ places ~ things ~ food ~ ~ books ~ smells ~ movies ~ activities

If you are yearning for more,
realize the only way you will receive it
is to be grateful for what you already have.

colors ~ people ~ places ~ things ~ food ~   ~ books ~ smells ~ movies ~ activities

colors ~ people ~ places ~ things ~ food ~   { 108 }   ~ books ~ smells ~ movies ~ activities

colors ~ people ~ places ~ things ~ food ~   { 109 }   ~ books ~ smells ~ movies ~ activities

colors ~ people ~ places ~ things ~ food ~ { 110 } ~ books ~ smells ~ movies ~ activities

Approach life with great *Z*eal!
Stay encouraged by surrounding yourself with other passionate and enthusiastic people.

colors ~ people ~ places ~ things ~ food ~   ~ books ~ smells ~ movies ~ activities

colors ~ people ~ places ~ things ~ food ~ ~ books ~ smells ~ movies ~ activities

colors ~ people ~ places ~ things ~ food ~   { 113 }   ~ books ~ smells ~ movies ~ activities

Observations

Take a minute to think about what you are thinking about.

Studies show that gratitude improves your relationships, your physical and psychological health as well as increasing your happiness. How has this journal impacted you? Write down your observations of how your life has been altered by increasing your gratitude.

colors ~ people ~ places ~ things ~ food ~ { 115 } ~ books ~ smells ~ movies ~ activities

colors ~ people ~ places ~ things ~ food ~ { **116** } ~ books ~ smells ~ movies ~ activities

colors ~ people ~ places ~ things ~ food ~ ~ books ~ smells ~ movies ~ activities

colors ~ people ~ places ~ things ~ food ~ { **118** } ~ books ~ smells ~ movies ~ activities

A	N
B	O
C	P
D	Q
E	R
F	S
G	T
H	U
I	V
J	W
K	X
L	Y
M	Z

colors ~ people ~ places ~ things ~ food ~   ~ books ~ smells ~ movies ~ activities

colors ~ people ~ places ~ things ~ food ~ { 120 } ~ books ~ smells ~ movies ~ activities

Made in the USA
Columbia, SC
28 December 2021